# DEFINITE
# SPACE

# DEFINITE
# SPACE

POEMS BY

## ANN IVERSON

HOLY COW! PRESS

DULUTH, MINNESOTA · 2007

The line "As by giving or letting go[?]" in "War Prayer"
is from Catherine Barnett's
*Into Perfect Spheres Such Holes Are Pierced*, Alice James Books 2004.
"Leafless. Coyotes." was written with assistance from
Margot Fortunato Galt

*Library of Congress Cataloging-in-Publication Data*

Iverson, Ann.
Definite space : poems / by Ann Iverson.
p. cm.
ISBN 978-0-9779458-4-9 (alk. paper)
I. Title.
PS3609.V47D44 2007
811'.6—dc22        2007010091

The author and publisher are grateful to Dunwoody College of Technology
(Minneapolis, Minnesota) for their generosity and support.

Holy Cow! Press books are distributed to the trade by
Consortium Book Sales & Distribution
c/o Perseus Distribution
1094 Flex Drive
Jackson, Tennessee 38301

This project is supported, in part, by a grant from the
Elmer L. & Eleanor J. Anderson Foundation and
by donations from generous individuals.

For personal inquiries, please write to:
Holy Cow! Press
Post Office Box 3170
Mount Royal Station, Duluth, Minnesota 55803

Please visit our website: www.holycowpress.org

*For Randy Jr.*

*&*

*Randy Sr.*


*For those who serve and*
*those who wait at home.*

I wish to thank the following individuals and establishments: Deborah Keenan for her assistance in manuscript arrangement; the Saturday morning poets (Carol Pearce Bjorlie, Teresa Boyer, Kirsten Dierking, Janet Jerve, Marie Richmeyer, Kathy Weihe, Liz Weir) for continued support and critique during the making of these poems; each member of the Laurel Poetry Collective for their joint inspiration; Hamline University for steady scholarship; Dunwoody College of Technology for their support and recognition; Shelly Leitheiser for her breathtaking cover art; cherished sisters (Margie, Claudia, Mary, Jean); dear friends and colleagues, near and afar, for their kindness towards and consideration for my art; and finally Jim Perlman and Rachel Lintula for believing in these poems.

# DEFINITE SPACE

## I

Twin Towers / 14

When a Son Goes Off to War / 16

Driving Through Louisiana, Christmas Day, 2002 / 17

What to Say / 19

The Yellow Ribbon / 20

Father of a Soldier / 21

Three A.M. First Call from Baghdad / 22

The Fourth of July, 2003 / 23

Aubade / 24

Too Close to Home, July 5th / 25

E-Mail / 26

Keep the Boy Alive / 27

Focus / 28

The Deployment: Ill at Ease / 29

Christmas Leave / 30

Incarcerated, Saddam Hussein Writes Poetry and Gardens / 31

Returning from NYC, November, 2001 / 32

Agenda of the Dead / 33

Half Moon at Christmas, 2001 / 34

Homecoming / 35

Post-Traumatic Stress / 36

War / 37

One Night Out of Many / 38

# II

Moving to the Country / 41

He Saw the Owl / 42

Her Job at Dusk While a Storm Threatens / 44

Homesick / 45

Politics in the Country / 46

Homesick, Again / 47

What Can Go Awry / 48

Anniversary / 49

Summer / 50

Sometimes if She Enters / 51

When You Sleep in November / 52

First Lesson / 53

Empty Nest / 54

Even Though / 55

Code in War Time / 56

Rooster Pheasant / 57

The New Garden / 58

Genesis / 59

Back to School / 60

# III

Summer's End / 63

Forgoing / 64

Falling, Rising, Sand / 65

No Promises Here / 66

Waiting for Winter / 67

The Second Deployment / 68

War Years are Like Animal Years / 69

Status Quo / 70

Peace / 71

Amazing How All Days Can Fall Into One / 72

Beside Himself / 73

Again, the Yellow Ribbon / 74

Before You Leave Again / 75

The Old Black Lab / 76

Existence / 77

Prayer / 78

God's Will / 79

Of Loneliness and Snow / 80

Leafless. Coyotes. / 81

Study: Shapes and Forms / 82

Alone After Christmas / 83

New Year's Day / 84

Milestone / 85

Sonnet for the Barren Birch / 86

Together We Planted Grass / 87

Count Down / 88

Now When She Drives / 89

War Prayer / 90

The Gift / 91

Acknowledgments / 92

About the Author, Her Stepson, and the Cover Artist / 93

This is a burning sun seen in a sky not here,
a landscape not on land as we know it.


*—Shelly Leitheiser, cover artist*

I

# TWIN TOWERS

*Left*

I move in this most definite space
and sometimes cannot save myself
from the comfort of order.

Towels and sheets folded neatly,
pillows aligned. Colors are on time
like the bills I always pay. I rewrite

lists and white out the names and
numbers of those I no longer need.
Punish myself if I change my mind.

*Right*


I feel definite in this most moving space
and wonder how it pulls me in and protects
from the world of structure.

Dust settles on the blinds; I overlook it
to see what's out the window. Colors
are not punctual but float in time.

I catch the names and numbers of those
I once admired like love falling from the sky.
I am wrong, wrong, wrongly in the right.

# WHEN A SON GOES OFF TO WAR

I walk out into the world alone at dusk
watch blackbirds with no strategic plan,
mission, or vision gather in the naked tree.

Hundreds of them fly in for this impromptu session,
where they put their wings together and form
an ark of shadow, a coalition between light and dark,
while from branches, decisions scatter in the air.

Filled with privilege like never before,
I open myself to the visual world
where doctrine and creed do not matter
so even God finds himself amongst

their turning eyes looking West,
knowing everything we long to know
about how light ends
and darkness has its way.

# DRIVING THROUGH LOUISIANA,
# CHRISTMAS DAY, 2002

All things silent then, the forest mindful in its worship while
abandoned trailers haunt the land and make vigil of lives

once led, together and at home. Armadillos hunker
between the shadows. From the back seat,
I count white wooden crosses.

What is here is everywhere: the irreversible, the small,
the insubordinate:
man, woman, son. The dog with a lowered head,
the barren tree. We travel

at a speed which works in a country waging war.
Which works for a boy in a military beret, his fate weighing in

on a curious scale that no small man can teeter. If it weren't
for the Live Oaks behind their veils of Spanish Moss, I might

not know what to believe in. Can I call ahead to save my place
with God? Our lives, small journeys that rise as quickly
as they fall.

I believe in the boy who drives so fast, I would not
recognize my life
if we passed it on the way.

So fast I don't recognize his worried brow
in the rearview mirror.
All untouchable subjects liquefy, pour out beyond the realms

of what can be contained.
Lets love spill best from broken hearts.

God, if there is a stream that does not empty
its pain into a larger world, teach my heart to learn its path.

# WHAT TO SAY

to a boy, soldier now
the last call home.

What to give
but a medal

of St. Christopher
whose burden too

was heavy:
a child

growing continually
with weight

across the raging stream
across the world

now resting on
his shoulders.

*Wear this medal*
we said to the boy,
soldier now.

# THE YELLOW RIBBON

She doesn't have an oak
so the giant pine will have to do.

It's not a ribbon either,
but a length of yellow tulle.

Her arms will hardly reach around,
though she relishes the imperfect gesture

as the heart clashes with the cliché.
When the clouds move in, she looks up

into the shooted shadows of branch,
her view of the world obstructed

by love and war. It's the only yellow
around an old pine tree that she can see,

as far as she will let herself look
down her simple-minded street,

un-ablazed with fire and bombs,
common, at peace, year after year.

# FATHER OF A SOLDIER

The sun leaves their house, their yard
and dark clouds transform themselves

into hydrangeas
just to find a purpose.

He bends towards the light
like an old lily planted in the shade,

draws in the great depths of his past.
Though it was not the sun he needed

that day he slammed into the house
threw the bags of groceries on the table

with the sight of a military vehicle
crouching near the home.

Incessantly, while she makes the bed,
pulls the weeds, puts on her makeup,

she hears a phone ringing
in her head.

# THREE A.M. FIRST CALL FROM BAGHDAD

Like screaming maniacs
we plummet
down the flight of stairs
could have easily broken
all of our legs.

The sharp pierce
of the ring's limited life
*find the phone*
*find the phone*
*where the fuck is the phone?*
*here it is*
*here it is*
then
your voice so sane.

# THE FOURTH OF JULY, 2003

She dreams
he returns from war
unscathed.
She dreams
they hug and kiss
so much
they all fall down
on the kitchen floor.
While there,
they blow warm air
into his mouth
until
his warrior-self
is melted
until
he is
a pool
of gleaming water.

# AUBADE

*When Edward Herrgott opened the door of their*
*home in Shakopee at 6:15 a.m. and saw two people*
*in U.S. Army uniform, he knew something was wrong.*
STAR TRIBUNE, July 5, 2003

The sun brings me a tray of yellow
a glass of orange
and promises.
But not until now
have I not believed them.

# TOO CLOSE TO HOME, JULY 5TH

You wept in line at the grocery store,
your shaking hands barely grasping
the news too close to home.
The photo of a family grief struck,
holding each other up
on their front porch.
I imagine you fumbled
for your check card,
your keys, your truck,
the road back to me
at the lake
waking slow,
heavy with dream
sweeping the porch
waiting for milk, bread,
cheese and eggs.

# E-MAIL

Wired nights,
unable to plug in
to the socket of sleep,
your father rises before dawn,
turns the computer on.

Invisible lines
carry invincible love,
one word at a time
over seven seas,
over skies, bright and muted.

Today you've been blown down,
an IED thrown
by a man in a donkey cart,
a boy by his side.
Your Hummer destroyed.

Your damaged ear
rings for days.
The printed message
trembles in your father's hands.

# KEEP THE BOY ALIVE

She ignites the fire
but he doesn't sit before it.
He prepares the food
but she doesn't eat.
She opens the book
yet neither read.

They keep the boy alive.
That's all they do night and day.

# FOCUS

He loses his glasses,
almost his mind,
screams about things
that don't matter.
She smokes cigarettes
stares out the window
until logic blurs away
into snowdrifts and newscasts.

Sometimes at night
she dreams of two people
near a cliff, two people
on the verge,
one small push.

# THE DEPLOYMENT: ILL AT EASE

*No* to everything in sight:
the slanted moon and pillared stars,

music making rainbows on the wall,
the heft of love and shadow.

*No* to the man in the moon
who needs his wife.

To sight and every leaning, naked tree,
to upright dreams, ambition.

## CHRISTMAS LEAVE

At the airport,
you are surrounded:
flags, signs,
embraces, cheers,
sobs, snapshots of
relief never having
again to drain from
human faces.

At the party,
Iraqi sand tracks the carpet,
a woman, exhausted,
whimpers in the hall.
Another tears up
at the sight of your boots
near the bed.

Days later, the cat
who only comes out for us
sprawls and rolls on her back
on the desk where you work.
So enamored with your presence,
she falls off the ledge,
so surprised by it all.

# INCARCERATED, SADDAM HUSSEIN WRITES POETRY AND GARDENS

Which makes me not want to do
either of the two again.
In one flash moment
I thought that I was the same as he,
caring for small unnoticed beauty.
The little words I write.
The modest flowers I cling to.

# RETURNING FROM NYC, NOVEMBER, 2001

I memorize pain and the shifting
of metal and concrete by sleeping

with the shades rolled up
to witness the dark world still turning.

You imagine what you love and hold it in your eyes,
but it rotates away in mirrors and shards of glass.

The silhouettes of two trees bend
into my window. One is so forceful

it pushes my heart to leap
from the fire within.

# AGENDA OF THE DEAD

It hovers.
Some fog on bad days

or a cape of monarchs
migrating towards a western sunset.

This is when it warms us,
the orange beauty of ten thousand wings.

The Aurora.
The Borealis.

It turns the skyline inside out,
so we can hold

the hands
that weave the sky.

# HALF MOON AT CHRISTMAS, 2001

When you're this kind of sad
light does this,

casts its shadow
against the bad.

Then unimaginable happiness
wedges in between the dark.

# HOMECOMING

The phone rings in the middle of the night,
a simple, steady voice:
*Hi Ann, I'm outside.*
*I thought I'd call first, so no one would shoot me.*
So the real story of his life begins.

# POST-TRAUMATIC STRESS

Stumbling drunk,
your father nearly
carries you to bed.

You sleep for hours,
wake up, case the dark hall,
shoulder up
arch your back
creep pass the open door,
where someone sleeps,
as though
it's another
fearful, shadowed passage.

# WAR

At lunch, people talk about it
here and there
between the weather
and their tuna sandwiches.
Between all the other losses
never mentioned
over Caesar salad
or beef stroganoff
or on an elevator
too slow
for its own good.

Speeding down County Road 18,
pouring rain, I saw light
beyond the clouds.
I talked to your image
rising from the mist
as though you make it through,
finding the solid truth
of God and blue sky.

# ONE NIGHT OUT OF MANY

Outrageous stars climb
the mountain of faith
and all we can do
is settle in
to the center
of the coyotes' howl.
What breadth
what indecision
what unison
bouncing from branch
to broken branch
they offer.
Though I do not
receive the word
*comfort*
even if
that is the intent.

II

# MOVING TO THE COUNTRY

It isn't the hundreds of starlings settling
in their startled ways
when the winds blow our star crossed love
off onto country roads so sad and beautiful.

It isn't the Sandhill Crane
cawing, swooping, estranged and
Pterodactyl-like
across the lonely fields of regret.

*When I am with you I feel alone.*
It doesn't matter who said it
or how the other replied.

Opposites attract,
so I stalk the house nude
looking out windows
to wide open space, in mirrors

to see if either the country or the body
would draw the heart in.
One cat shakes his head in disapproval.

It might be the wind, serendipitous
or the birch mocking a familiar sky.
Thoughts of the old life brew
disorder in a mind.

It isn't for your correction:
*swallows not starlings.*
I want them to be starlings, of course,
and this love to be aligned.

# HE SAW THE OWL

and all she saw
were tangled branches.

No pivoting head.
No froth of feathers.

She saw the deer,
but let him see them first

as though it were a game
that she would never win.

In his peripheral sight
he envisions her life

thinks to himself
now she's writing

she must be happy.
Now she's painting

she must be happy.
Now she's wrapping

gifts in all their glitter
of red and gold.

*She must be happy*
he says aloud

but never really does.
He sees the roads at night

and all she sees is darkness.
When she dreams,

he sees nothing.
Those roads don't belong to him.

# HER JOB AT DUSK WHILE A STORM THREATENS

The earth gathers what she can:
rabbit, doe, turkey, pheasant,
mallard, birch, sand, pine, and fox.

Lets go of clover and tulip,
of oak, weasel, cattail,
the brown-eyed conundrum of forest,
the murky complacency
of water.

Picks up, as she flees,
crickets one by one.
Sweeps up the dull
center of mud.
Tucks in the corners
of uprooted elm.

Devours petunia,
daisy, not the rose,
no never the rose,
snake and fire.
So thirsty, swallows the pond
in one gulp.

Wants to steal lark,
finch, blue jay, rainbow,
shadows of oak
pressed against the sky.

# HOMESICK

Harrowing between the indisputable moon
and the consequences of the sky,
you find yourself in a new place
where roads are not familiar
where roots ascend
into trees that push counterfeit leaves
between birds who sing songs
you don't know the words to.

# POLITICS IN THE COUNTRY

Pretend the birch at dusk are people
with only something nice to say.

And the crow perched
on the long neck of corn

is a campaign commercial
that flies out of your mind

as soon as you turn the channel.
Imagine the cattle and geese

voiceless and what a break
that might be

when everything is talking at once.
Quiet Moon,

gleaming best among the stars,
where do *you* stand on these issues?

# HOMESICK, AGAIN

The birds in their obsequious songs
trick me into believing in the country.

It only lasts for hours
on this perfect spring day.

Then I stand up from the lawn chair
as dusk rolls in

nod my head to agree with the lofty clouds
that I have been deceived.

# WHAT CAN GO AWRY

I thought about leaving you
many times today

moving back to the city
where the roads are lit,

the Moon so insignificant,
stars an addendum.

Many times today
I did not question

the crux of your shadow
knitted to mine

in the deepness of night
when our bodies

form a pattern on the wall.
Instead, I only moved

from room to room,
teetered on the cusp

of what breaks away
or falls.

# ANNIVERSARY

See how the night finally turns to forgive?

And the stars, undertakers
for all the death in love, do not look away.

It is not the death of anything tonight
though the mind may wander.

The roads are free and clear.

Yet the sky hedges formidable shapes,
resembles sorrows you try to forget.

,     ,     ,

See how meanings change yet words remain the same?

And the moon, midwife to
all the birth in love, guides with blazing light.

We crown again,
an anointed definition

compelled to carry on.

We take the shapes and mold them
into something we can be.

# SUMMER

is an ocean in which I swim.
For days I do not see land,
a white haze, a blurry border.

In summer I walk like a flower would
if it could and stationary thoughts
find motion. I've told you enough

of the sorrows already. Believe me
summer burns in northern hearts while
light diminishes one minute a day.

Gradations of dusk follow the path.
A woman asleep in her bed tosses and turns
that the stars won't mark her way.

# SOMETIMES IF SHE ENTERS

the perimeter of fear
as a doe at dusk
crossing the ragged border
of birch and swamp
into the human clearing
where instead she finds
slices of apple or banana
and a woman in a window
softly cooing a made up name,
quietly planning a different life,
looking eye to eye, the invincibility
of what lurks beyond and calls
and never disappoints.
If only *she* could cross the border
and she has.

# WHEN YOU SLEEP IN NOVEMBER

A woman of dark trees
hovers near your bed
gathers your dreams
pockets those missing.
In great bushels
she stores them.

For your lacking days
every dream is in
her branches,
her leafy garment
you take away

to touch the underside
of her warmest belly
nipples from pure earth
dark folds beyond this hunting thing.

You think about her
when I'm talking
my futile chatter.
I try saying
*don't go away so long*

to her darkness
which you say is mine.
And aren't we all alike
we women and
our secret places?

# FIRST LESSON

The doe teaches fear to her fawn
in the barren back lot.
She explains
ease of mistrust
necessity of suspect.
She whispers
*doubt everything*
*watch me as I tilt my ears*
*and quiver.*

# EMPTY NEST

Two robins sing sad songs so softly
that even the leaves cannot chime in.

Neither bird can hear the inaudible
music that the other makes, separated

by their habitual ways in a nest that suddenly
appears overly spacious over night.

If the birds were human
driving through the fields

of northern Minnesota,
though each bird speechless,

the other wonders
if the other heard.

# EVEN THOUGH

neither of the horses trotted to the fence
when I clicked my tongue and sang,

nor did the sun appear when I whistled,
stayed lurking in the loft.

I snapped my fingers, but the murky day
would not pass,

clapped my hands at pheasants in the sky,
but their plane would not reverse.

I cleared my throat and raised my voice,
though the city did not respond.

And the soldiers stay away too long,
for years and years and years

Even though we call to them.
Even though they hear.

# CODE IN WAR TIME

He has never heard her cry
like she cries in the country,
complete and unutterable sobs.
Water that shakes her body,
walls, foundation, the last leaves
of shimmering birch.

Wild turkeys scatter.
Downy geese flush south.
Cats come searching.
Dogs howl, upset by the upset.

She runs her fingers over his sign:
Giant man tears dripping
down the moonlit hall
before dawn.

# ROOSTER PHEASANT

comes with a *squawk, squawk*
so distinct, almost human
that I've learned to listen well enough
to know when he finally clears the woods,
reaches the corn feed
which my husband
lovingly or desperately
scattered at the edge,
hoping that if wild life came in the spring,
I would finally stop missing the city.

He enters with a gait so blazingly self-guided,
I begin to recognize that my mediocrity
and doubts are good, are good
if I can watch him strut his life
here and again,
now and for a while.

# THE NEW GARDEN

sits alone at dusk
after the human retires

to predictable walls,
steaming bath water,

echoes of a baseball game.
The new garden does not mind being

alone at night, though no one ever asks.
And kind of enjoys being the only sign

of organized beauty out here
where the wild takes it cruel, haphazard course.

But the new garden stirs at night
in a bed of sage, ageratum,

alyssum, sedum, when she hears
the tiny, distant screams of death.

# GENESIS

Creatures shriek in arbitrary death;
tiny phantoms rise from swamp and brush
when three days of insistent rain resides.

The half-way moon is not accountable tonight
and the doe slides into the boat
as easily as out.

More simplistically and more common
the trees raise victorious tongues.

God rides by on a barge of clouds.

There's a small spot of sun on the kitchen floor,
but Memory in her apron can't bear to sweep it up.

# BACK TO SCHOOL

What does one doe do,
spying from the corridor
of leaf and branch,
with hope so intense?
Her two fawn making friends
with the woman who
gently slides open the screen door,
steps quietly and indiscreetly
on the grasses of
some far off dream
she's had for years.

III

# SUMMER'S END

The hibiscus grows seven faces.
You check yourself in the mirror,
find only two.

That's one too many.
Lose one by the light of the moon.

A bat flies loose through the house
at night. You think it's your dark side
trying to find you.

Don't tell the sun
where his last ray is.
He'll leave it without it anyway.

You've been so happy here in this gracious light,
putting things away, where no one,
not even you, can find them.

# FOREGOING

I love your sound on my voice mail.
It spreads through me as yellow
through trees in heady October.

It positions itself directly, just near my heart
with neither love nor hate, but commonness
as you speak to me when I can't talk back.

Your voice is different,
drifts away into a singular boat
on an amber river.

# FALLING, RISING, SAND

Help the fallen soldiers up
that they might lift themselves
from sand
and the dark calls of desert sky.

May they rise
again and again and again
from blood and roadside bombs,
to good homes and street lights,
apple pie and MTV,
the Fourth of July
traced out in silent sparks
between heaven
and before
the news arrives.

# NO PROMISES HERE

Not tonight,
when the chorus frogs sing
their murkish notes
and the sun finally
delegates light to the moon.

*No promises here* I say
that I will stay
as darkness settles into the land
while the son leaves again
for war.

# WAITING FOR WINTER

If darkness has another name
I call it *Impatient* or *Just Get Here.*

*Brooding Too Soon* will
not do for this baptism

of gray and brown,
black in its epitome of black,

a completely collapsed yellow
in a pot on the stoop.

The swallows old nest,
empty, messy, crackling,

as I hose it down,
thinking about a friend's

husband, the tumor.
unidentified.

You bless *One More Winter*
in the country.

I christen it
*I Don't Believe You.*

# THE SECOND DEPLOYMENT

weeks before the second deployment we tighten as a ratchet twisting and grinding and twisting and grinding until there is no relief from the pressure no respite from the weight no reprieve from the demand of that which we have no say during which I have no choice but to coil my eyes to uninvited tears clench my teeth to un-sought words in which I make a life of unsolic-ited dreams and watch you pace and pace and pace although you are going nowhere and in circles we continue and in a square we will begin.

# WAR YEARS ARE LIKE ANIMAL YEARS

From an airtight window
in the perfect new house

I watch you
rip and lunge

through weed and sand,
rev the engine loud and mean,

lean in. Take curves around me,
powerless, alone

in the window, tight.
As you circle around

again and again,
I get dizzy, sit down

think *this can't be happening again.*
You are not 21 but 147.

## STATUS QUO

Together we throw your clothes
into the machine.

I reach while saying
*There's soap in the cupboard.*

You say *these are my hurricane clothes:*
Back from Rita, off again to war.

# PEACE

Four young men weep:
Clayton
John
Nick
Randy.
Brothers of childhood
in arms.
Such a vigilant message—
Liturgical art
scrolling down faces,
stunning and stained glass.

# AMAZING HOW ALL DAYS CAN FALL INTO ONE

You are home you are gone you are home you are gone.
I-can-no-longer-distinguish-the-hours-of-your-passing-and-coming.

And your father? His oblivion becomes out of sorts, trespasses
even the boundaries of his sentences: curt now, business only.

# BESIDE HIMSELF

That's what she answers
when someone asks about
your father.

Two words for one man
torn in half, the second
looking curious and sad—
again this sudden arrangement.

She too,
looks to the other self,
and actually calls out to the detached.

Yet,
for all that can be
accomplished
between four people,

nothing happens here tonight.

# AGAIN, THE YELLOW RIBBON

Frayed and soiled from the wind,
sand of that year,

you take it from the carved oak trunk
he sent last time as a house-warming gift,

tear off one of the very tattered streams.
I think why? Then think to rinse

the whole bow off. But no.
To honor the piece gone missing,

I put it back into the trunk.
What blows away, returns.

# BEFORE YOU LEAVE AGAIN

We gather for dinner,
good friends and all.

We push the big bowl aside
to make room for plates and napkins.

The cat, you know the one,
jumps up and curls into the bowl.

We talk and laugh and joke
though no one says a word.

# THE OLD BLACK LAB

Remembers you
leans on you
licks you
cherishes

*You*

in your sandy fatigues.

Waits faithfully outside
the bathroom as you shower

would scrub your back
hold the towel
part the sea,

*anything*
imaginable, unimaginable
just to keep you home.

# EXISTENCE

Animals search me every day
for the answer in my eyes.

I have nothing to say
to the dog in the sun,

to the cats on the walk,
to the sun streaming in.

A cumulative sentence or two,
loose words, main idea up front.

Then periodic combinations to build
us up and up towards meaning.

# PRAYER

Small it seems when versing in my mind.
Half way through I pause, though
I need to send one up.
I come to a huge body of water and wait.

,       ,       ,

The sky itself is an intervention between
words and heart. So the heart is a rosary,
each bead a beat towards light.

,       ,       ,

I am not down on my knees.
My hands are not folded.

,       ,       ,

I do what is possible within the confinement
of my own heart flowing-out-beyond-
what-is-doable-and-undoable.
I reverse every one I've ever said as though
I've planted it upside down
but it makes its way to light, regardless.

# GOD'S WILL

If God would give me word
it would be the reflection
of a young man on my street.

Between two panes of opposite glass
he is walking, ablazed,
forwards, backwards
towards me and away.

# OF LONELINESS AND SNOW

The streaming light
of ambivalence

as the snow beguiles
all the windows of this town.

Snow people walk past mine,
utter a billion promises.

I hear only white,
not the red of death

or the blue of birth.
I touch the headlights

of one lone car making its way
through the white canal.

Snow storm, pull me from
your whited ways.

Befriend me.

## LEAFLESS. COYOTES.

I will not walk out past the border of trees
into thickets and tall grasses, laden
with frantic gnashing, for fear
I will find what I've already heard:
the womp and swallow of tongue and teeth.

The harvest moon hides
in the distant calligraphy of branch,
climbs, then hides again, does not know
what to do with me now
that she owns me
out here in the country.

# STUDY: SHAPES AND FORMS

Yesterday, triangular,
another point we never met.

Last night a circle,
the finishing—
the unfinished.

Business oblong
like you and the black lab

stretched out and calling
for another body to make it tri-

symmetrical on the couch.
The faded moon behind
and perpendicular.

# ALONE AFTER CHRISTMAS

The collective mind
of snowflakes
help me gather
strength
to make the earth
a friend of snow.

A gentle face
against a lonesome wood
and blanched sky,
something to believe in.

The black lab eats the carrot nose.
I tire so and thus the person small.

Though each flake
states its case of beauty,
hides and will dissolve again
into something
greater than the ordinary.

# NEW YEAR'S DAY

Melancholy orbits dash away a sun.
Children skate on the cleared and silky pond.

The man stokes a fire on the field.
My favorite cat clears my lap

like I was a thought
he was tired of having.

For better or for worse
we both agreed.

Now, agreeing
for the better.

# MILESTONE

When the heart is at peace
at the place of everlasting,
comes as it does
as the moon through the trees.
With light, knowledge.
Shadows cast yesterday
are only deer talking
in the woods behind your heart.
Beams of darkness thrust through
the long sleeves of your life
become hands that are not empty.

# SONNET FOR THE BARREN BIRCH

Every morning when I wash my hair
This barren birch, which I've grown to love,
Looks in on me at dawn as I wait for water
To run warm, lather, rinse, repeat.

At windswept noon, as I slice the cheese
For crackers, it sways an inosculation
Of arteries and life, each intimate
Road and limb, an answer in an answer.

A halo of beaded moon it wears
As I scan its twilight heart and
Weepy silhouette, listen to the news,
Dry the cups and plates and saucers.

At midnight, I wake it from its fruitless sleep
To ask another question.

# TOGETHER WE PLANTED GRASS

By tractor, hand, and body,
we pulled peculiar, encumbering growth,
sticker weeds,
wild flowers and brush
as tall and big as me.

You tilled the sandy acreage
and finally spread the seed.
I followed behind
with the miracle of green,
careful, then careful again
to hit the missed and lonely
spots you graded with a rake.

Finally tired,
I tossed handfuls to the wind
like rice at a wedding.
*Congratulations!*
*Best wishes!*
As though
everyone we knew
was happy
in their marriage.

# COUNT DOWN

Every morning she wakes
relieved again.


    Silence


Only the collective sounding
of geese migration,
the giant roar of Highway 65.

Though the Great Blue Heron
hunkered in the tails
utters not a word.

And the swaying oaks
are hushed
in morning prayer

while bumble bees buzz with dramatics
in the Russian Sage.
She cannot hear their urgent message.

Still sleepy, she cannot hear a single sound,

Nor the imagined engine trolling up the drive.
Nor the doorbell ringing with bad news.

Oh . . . she thinks, half awake
of those must who carry that burden.

# NOW WHEN SHE DRIVES

she barely sees the blur of road,
floats over decision
turn the music louder, louder,
softer, louder.

Deer leap decisively into destruction.
That's how it appears
when the sound is mute.

She begins to tally road kill.
Why wouldn't she count the dead
or recognize a pattern?

Cumulative thoughts swell:
pay the bills, hire teachers, send a card,
see the doctor, call your sister.
The English Setter's tumor grows
finally past the limit.

Yes, *past the limit*
exactly as he said.

# WAR PRAYER

How to mend the wounds?
As by giving or letting go?

How to end the never-ending story?
The story rendering the never-ended.

Time floats in its own accordance,
destiny doubles and breaks into bloom,

fire and destruction, history and loss.
The world tilts, we slide with it.

But see the goslings follow in the pond?
They grow, depart, return.

The boy, man now, more and more
*will* go on forever.

# THE GIFT

I cry now at the simplest of things.
The May Day basket
of pink, yellow, and green construction paper
hung on our front door.
Its message:
*To: a good neighbor*
*From: Farnsworth Kindergarten Room 106*
On the handle, the artist's signature
in purple and red crayon, *Ashley Langhess.*
The crooked, paper torn petals and trunk like stems.
Its lopsided loveliness.
I tape it to the fridge.

## ACKNOWLEDGMENTS

The author would like to thank the editors of the following publications where these poems have appeared or are forthcoming, sometimes in a slightly different form.

"Twin Towers"  *Margie: The American Journal of Poetry,* 2002

"When a Son Goes off to War"  *Oklahoma Review,* 2004

"Driving Through Louisiana, Christmas Day, 2002"  *Conte,* Winter 2006

"What to Say"  *Poetry East #62,* 2008

"The Yellow Ribbon"  *Bombshells: War Stories and Poems by Women on the Homefront,* (Omni Arts, LLC, 2007)

"Father of a Soldier"  *Poetry East #62,* 2008

"Three A.M. First Call From Baghdad"  *Conte,* Winter 2006

"Agenda of the Dead"  *Echoes from the Heart: September 11th Anthology,* 2003

"The Fourth of July, 2003"  *Pulling for Good News,* Spring 2004

"Aubade"  *Poetry East #62,* 2008

"Her Job at Dusk While a Storm Threatens"  *Blue Earth Review,* Spring 2006

"Sometimes if She Enters"  *Cezanne's Carrot,* 2006

"When You Sleep in November"  *Oklahoma Review,* 2004

"Homesick, Again"  *Talking Stick,* "Choices" 2006

"Politics in the Country"  *Ignite,* Spring 2006

"Homesick"  *Tarwolf Review,* Winter/Spring 2005

"Back to School"  *Cezanne's Carrot,* Spring 2006

"Prayer"  *BlueFire* and *Blue Earth Review,* Summer 2005

"Milestone"  *Cezanne's Carrot,* Spring 2006

"Sonnet to the Barren Birch"  *Love Letters,* February 2005

"Alone After Christmas"  *Kritya* 2006

"New Year's Day"  *Kritya* 2006

"Study: Shapes and Forms"  *Kritya* 2006

ANN IVERSON received her MALS and MFA from Hamline University. She is the author of *Come Now to the Window,* Laurel Poetry Collective. Her writing has been featured on The Writer's Almanac with Garrison Keillor and has appeared or is forthcoming in *The Oklahoma Review, Margie: American Journal of Poetry, Poetry East, Water-Stone Review* and others. A visual artist, Ann takes interest in the intuitive and cyclical exchanges made between language and image. Her artwork debuted at the Undercroft Gallery at St. Matthew's Episcopal Church in St. Paul. She currently is the Senior Academic Director of Arts and Sciences at Dunwoody College of Technology in Minneapolis. She and her husband live in East Bethel, Minnesota.

SERGEANT RANDY IVERSON JR. enlisted in the United States Army in June of 2002. He served two tours of duty in Baghdad as a Military Police officer and a personal bodyguard and aide for the commander of the 519th Military Police Battalion. Randy is the recipient of several combat awards and is decorated with numerous medals, including two Army Commendation medals. He recently completed military police canine training. Randy re-enlisted and will serve in some capacity until 2010.

SHELLY LEITHEISER (cover artist) is a painter, published photographer, and digital artist who lives in central Minnesota. Her work has won several awards at local art shows. Her paintings are primarily in watercolors and acrylic, and she is influenced by many portrait and surrealist artists. She is currently exploring how technology can enhance the creative process, by merging traditional painting with digital images. More of her work can be found at www.revolutionaryart.org.